Breaking Out of Isolation

CORWIN CONNECTED EDUCATORS SERIES

Content Curation for Educators
By Steven W. Anderson @web20classroom

5 Powerful Skills for the Global Learner
By Mark Barnes @markbarnes19

Teaching the iStudent: A Quick Guide to Using Mobile Devices and Social Media in the K–12 Classroom
By Mark Barnes @markbarnes19

Digital Citizenship
By Susan Bearden

Connected Leadership: It's Just a Click Away
By Spike Cook @DrSpikeCook

Breaking Out of Isolation
By Spike C. Cook @DrSpikeCook, Jessica Johnson @PrincipalJ, and Theresa Stager @PrincipalStager

All Hands on Deck: Tools for Connecting Educators, Parents, and Communities
By Brad Currie @bradmcurrie

Standing in the Gap: Resources for Connecting New Teachers
By Lisa Dabbs @teachwithsoul and Nicol Howard @NicolRHoward

Missing Voices of EdTech Conversations
By Rafranz Davis @RafranzDavis

Flipping Leadership Doesn't Mean Reinventing the Wheel
By Peter DeWitt @PeterMDeWitt

The Edcamp Model: Powering Up Professional Learning
By the Edcamp Foundation @EdcampUSA

Worlds of Making: Best Practices for Establishing a Makerspace for Your School
By Laura Fleming @NMHS_lms

Personalized Learning Plans for Teachers
By Tom Murray @thomascmurray and Jeff Zoul @Jeff_Zoul

Empowered Schools, Empowered Students: Creating Connected and Invested Learners
By Pernille Ripp @pernilleripp

Blogging for Educators: Tips for Getting Connected
By Starr Sackstein @mssackstein

Principal PD
By Joseph Sanfelippo @Joesanfelippofc and Tony Sinanis @TonySinanis

The Power of Branding: Telling Your School's Story
By Tony Sinanis @TonySinanis and Joseph Sanfelippo @Joesanfelippofc

The Educator's Guide to Creating Connections
Edited by Tom Whitby @tomwhitby

The Relevant Educator: How Connectedness Empowers Learning
By Tom Whitby @tomwhitby and Steven W. Anderson @web20classroom

Breaking Out of Isolation

Becoming a Connected School Leader

Spike C. Cook
Jessica Johnson
Theresa Stager

CORWIN
A SAGE Company

A SAGE Company

FOR INFORMATION:

Corwin

A SAGE Company

2455 Teller Road

Thousand Oaks, California 91320

(800) 233-9936

www.corwin.com

SAGE Publications Ltd.

1 Oliver's Yard

55 City Road

London EC1Y 1SP

United Kingdom

SAGE Publications India Pvt. Ltd.

B 1/I 1 Mohan Cooperative Industrial Area

Mathura Road, New Delhi 110 044

India

SAGE Publications Asia-Pacific Pte. Ltd.

3 Church Street

#10-04 Samsung Hub

Singapore 049483

Copyright © 2016 by Corwin

Printed in the United States of America

ISBN 978-1-4833-9242-4

This book is printed on acid-free paper.

Acquisitions Editor: Ariel Price

Editorial Assistant: Andrew Olson

Production Editor: Amy Joy Schroller

Copy Editor: Lana Todorovic-Arndt

Typesetter: C&M Digitals (P) Ltd.

Proofreader: Rae-Ann Gordon

Cover Designer: Janet Kiesel

Marketing Manager: Lisa Lysne

SUSTAINABLE FORESTRY INITIATIVE

Certified Chain of Custody
Promoting Sustainable Forestry
www.sfiprogram.org
SFI-01268

SFI label applies to text stock

15 16 17 18 19 10 9 8 7 6 5 4 3 2 1

Contents

Preface   ix

About the Authors   xii

Introduction   1

1. On an Island by Yourself   2

      What Is Isolation, and How Does It Impact You?   5
      Professional Learning   6
      Pitfalls   7
      Conclusion   9
         Reflection and Action   10

2. Finding Your Professional Learning Network   11

      Connection!   14
      Establishing a PLN   18
      It's About Building Relationships   21
      Starting Your Own PLN   23
      Educator Spotlight—*Christopher Nesi*   24
      Conclusion   25
         Reflection and Action   26

3. Maintaining Balance   27

      What Connected Administrators Have To Say   30
      Why You Might Feel More Isolated   34
      Educator Spotlight—*Shawna Miller*   35
      Becoming the Linchpin   36
      Conclusion   37
         Reflection and Action   38

4. Embracing Isolation and Connection With Mindset   40

    What Is Mindset?   41

    Isolated by Principle   43

    Connected by Principle   45

    Educator Spotlight—*Jay Posick*   47

    Conclusion   48

    Reflection and Action   49

5. Now What? So What? What's Next?   50

    Now What? So What?   51

    How Can Your New Learning
        Help You Grow as a Leader?   52

    What's Next for You?   53

    Spotlight—*Brad Gustafson*   54

    Conclusion   56

    Reflection and Action   57

Resource: People We Follow and Why   59

References   63

Preface

My best friend is a high school math teacher. When I started working on the Corwin Connected Educators series, I excitedly told her about the power of using social media to connect with other educators. I passed on what I learned from the authors in this series: that the greatest resource educators have is each other. At a conference, she heard Jennie Magiera speak and finally made the leap to getting on Twitter. Although I wasn't sure she would continue tweeting, she did, and even joined Twitter chats like #connectedtl and #slowmathchat. A few days later, she texted me saying, "I seriously cannot thank you enough. You have changed my life."

Being "connected" seems deceptively simple: Just get on Twitter, right? But that's really not enough. For those who truly embrace connectedness, it's a lifestyle change, an openness to sharing and learning in an entirely new environment. We're seeing the impact of this shift in mindset worldwide. Policies are changing, new jobs in education are being created, hitherto impossible collaborations are happening, pedagogy is evolving, and there's a heightened awareness of each person's individual impact. All of these changes are explored in the Connected Educators series.

While you can see the full list of books on the series page, we're introducing several new books to the series; they will be published in the fall of 2015 and spring of 2016. These books each contribute something unique and necessary not only for educators who are new to the world of connected education, but also for those who have been immersed in it for some time.

Tom Whitby, coauthor of *The Relevant Educator*, has brought together a group of experienced connected educators in his new book, *The Educator's Guide to Creating Connections*. Contributors Pam Moran, George Couros, Kyle Pace, Adam Bellow, Lisa Nielsen, Kristen Swanson, Steven Anderson, and Shannon McClintock Miller discuss the ways that connectedness has impacted them and the benefits it can have for all educators—policy makers, school and district leaders, and teachers.

While all connected educators are evangelists for being connected, connectedness does not necessarily prevent common problems, such as isolation in leadership. In *Breaking Out of Isolation*, Spike Cook, Jessica Johnson, and Theresa Stager explain how connectedness can alleviate the loneliness leaders can feel in their position and also, when used effectively, help leaders maintain balance in their lives and stay motivated.

For districts and schools embracing the connected mindset and empowering all of their learners to use technology, a solid plan for digital citizenship is a must. In *Digital Citizenship*, Susan Bearden provides a look at how leaders can prepare teachers and students for the new responsibilities of using technology and interacting with others on a truly global platform.

Connected education provides unique opportunities for teachers in their classrooms as well. In *Standing in the Gap*, Lisa Dabbs and Nicol Howard explore the ways that social media can specifically help new teachers find resources, connect to mentors, and encourage each other in their careers. Erin Klein, Tom Murray, A. J. Juliani, and Ben Gilpin show how teachers can purposefully integrate technology and empower their students in both physical and digital classrooms in *Redesigning Learning Spaces*.

One of the most powerful impacts connected education can have is in reaching marginalized populations. In *Confident Voices*, John Spencer shows how social media and other technology tools can empower English language learners. Billy Krakower and Sharon LePage Plante have also discovered that technology can reach special and gifted learners as well.

The books in the Corwin Connected Educators series are supported by a companion website featuring videos, articles, downloadable forms, and other resources to help you as you start and continue your journey. Best of all, the authors in the series want to connect with *you*! We've provided their Twitter handles and other contact information on the companion website.

Once you've taken the step to joining a network, don't stop there. Share what you're doing; you never know when it will help someone else!

—*Peter DeWitt, Series Editor*
@PeterMDeWitt

—*Ariel Price, Associate Editor*
@arielkprice

About the Authors

 **Spike C. Cook** is the principal at RM Bacon Elementary School in Millville, New Jersey. He is a lifelong learner who enjoys collaborating with other educators throughout the world to improve teaching and learning.

As a new administrator, Dr. Cook used social media to transform his leadership into a 21st century mindset. He built the technology capacity within his school so that teachers, parents, and students can connect with others throughout the globe. He is the cocreator of the participant-driven professional development "unconference" model called "Tech Fridays" at his school and works collaboratively with other administrators to promote 21st century learning. Spike is committed to assisting and learning from other educators.

Spike was featured in Eric Sheninger's best-selling book *Digital Leadership*. In Chapter 3, Eric Sheninger captured Spike's keys to sustainable change in his school. Spike is also the cofounder of the popular *Principalcast*, a weekly round table podcast on educational tech and pedagogy. He has presented at the Association for Supervision and Curriculum Development (ASCD) and the National Association of Elementary School Principals (NAESP) national conferences, as well as at state and local conferences.

Spike earned a bachelor's degree, two master's degrees, and a doctorate from Rowan University. He is currently an adjunct professor at Rowan University in the College of Education where he teaches aspiring administrators in the Master's of School Administration. He lives in Turnersville, New Jersey, with his wife Theresa and two children, Henry and Catherine.

Spike's blog Insights Into Learning was recognized as a finalist for Best Administrator Blog by the EduBlog Awards in 2013. Connect with @drspikecook via Twitter.

Jessica Johnson is an elementary school principal and district assessment coordinator for Dodgeland School District in Juneau, Wisconsin. She is the 2014 Wisconsin Elementary School Principal of the Year. She has previously taught in Minnesota, where she earned her bachelor of arts degree at Bemidji State University. She also taught and worked as an instructional coach and assistant principal in Arizona, earning her master's degree at Arizona State University. As a continuing learner, she is passionate about literacy, principal productivity, social media, technology integration, and the concept of leading with a "coaching hat" as an administrator. She has a self-published children's novel *Adventures in Blockworld: A Novel for the Young Minecraft Fans*. She comoderates the #educoach chat on Twitter each Wednesday night at 9pm CST and also cohosts the PrincipalPLN Podcast. You can follow Jessica on Twitter as @PrincipalJ, follow her blog at principalj .net, or contact her at jessica@principalj.net.

Theresa Stager earned her bachelor of music education degree from Wayne State University in Detroit, Michigan, in 2003 and a master in educational administration (assessment and evaluation) degree at University of Michigan-Dearborn in 2007. She taught for 8 years as a public school music educator teaching general music, band, and high school choir. She worked for 2 years as an implementation director at a human resources company until

2013. Theresa has presented at many music, administration, and technology conferences in her career. Her music education blog was nominated and chosen as one of the Top 75 eCollegeFinder Music and Arts Enthusiasts Award Winners. Theresa was featured in Dr. Spike Cook's first book *Connected Leadership: It's Just a Click Away.*

Theresa is a cohost of PrincipalPLN podcast that can be found at principalpln.com and on iTunes. She is currently in her 2nd year as lead learner and building principal at St. Mary Catholic School in Rockwood, Michigan. She has implemented a one-to-one iPad program and is excited to be able to merge her love of technology, learning, and education with this position. She lives in Huron Township, Michigan, with husband Brian and two children, Audrey and Jacob. Theresa believes her biggest professional accomplishment is yet to come.

Introduction

G etting connected is one thing, and many educators are taking the plunge to become connected. Once connected, how does the leader avoid the isolation inherent in leadership? We have learned from conversations with others that many educators need help balancing their connected journey and working with their peers. Our book is intended to be a resource to ensure that the leadership wheels do not fall off when you are connected or isolated.

We—Spike, Jessica, and Theresa—have been connected to one another via Twitter for nearly 3 years. Despite living in three different states and two different time zones, we have used the power of social media tools to connect on a regular basis, record over 50 podcasts, and write a book while never meeting together in the same physical space. Despite our distance, we consider one another to be friends and close colleagues who call upon each other to survive the isolation that is inherent in school leadership.

On an Island
by Yourself

"Isolation was designed by our educational system."

—Seth Godin

School leadership can be a very challenging path. Often times, school leaders feel isolated from their peers, teachers, and community because they have to balance an endless list of responsibilities. Who can school leaders go to if they want to vent, ask questions, or propose an idea? Can they find someone objective and not steeped in the decision-making process? By using social media, school leaders can expand their world and connect with other like-minded individuals throughout the globe. This book will focus on the leadership isolation that plagues many school leaders. Throughout the book, the reader will be presented with vignettes from school leaders, as well as practical activities designed to help overcome leadership isolation. As the reader embarks on the learning embedded in the book, they will be able to easily implement their learning for others to see. In addition, the reader will be able to overcome the isolation associated with leadership by using tools to become connected. The timing of this book lends itself to the growing presence of school leaders using social media to empower themselves and others that coincides with the increased demands on their leadership.

How can anyone feel alone when they work with people? This is the conundrum of the modern world. In schools, we are in constant contact with teachers, parents, students, and community members, and yet we feel isolated? There are many reasons for this feeling of isolation, and there is a lot of work that needs to be done in order to help combat isolation. But first, we need to understand that there is a problem before we can work to solve it.

For instance, whenever Jessica Johnson presents along with her fellow Wisconsin principals, Curt Rees, Jay Posick, and Matt Renwick, on the topic of connected administrators, they use Gilligan's Island as their theme, because administrators often feel as if they are on an island. Their slides have humorous pictures from the infamous TV show with questions such as "If all your advice came from the same small group of people, or no one at all, where would you be?" Many educators, without knowing it, are living on an island with many questions and no one to ask.

Jessica and her Wisconsin counterparts coined the term *Gilligan Syndrome*, which can apply to any educator, not just administrators. Gilligan Syndrome occurs when you find yourself stuck because you do not have valuable resources when you really need them. Ask yourself now, "Who do you to turn to for advice and help?" Perhaps it is a trusted colleague, possibly someone you met at a conference, or maybe it is your spouse. How often do you feel stuck as a result of going to the same people time after time? It is easy to become stranded and not know how or who to reach out to for help.

According to Fullan and Hargraeves (1996), as much as schools are seeking to improve, many educators are experiencing frustration, isolation, and increased demands. There have been other studies that have also echoed this sentiment regarding isolation in school leadership (Beaudoin & Taylor, 2004; Cookson, 2005; Dussault & Thibodeau, 1997; Garmston, 2007). If isolation persists, according to Stephenson and Bauer (2010), it can lead to burnout and poor quality of work. How can this be?

Even in large districts where leaders may be part of a system with many schools, they still feel that once they are in their school, it is like no other schools exist. There are many causes to becoming isolated. Unfortunately many principals report that they cannot trust their colleagues or feel the top-down pressure from their district to lead their school to have the highest achievement scores, preventing them from sharing, and still others are just not willing to share ideas. There are principals who, despite their best efforts, are unable to gather momentum after a local, state, or even national conference when they have met people who are like-minded. Generally speaking, they return to their school or district and have difficulty finding the time to call or e-mail their new-found counterparts.

When Jessica worked with a group of new administrators in her state, an assistant principal reluctantly shared her frustrations with the situation she was in. As the assistant principal shared the issues with Jessica, she indicated that there was no collaboration between the other assistant principals. In taking the job, she assumed it would be a team effort. Yet, the principal had divided them into supervision of different grade levels (a common practice in buildings with multiple administrators).This, in addition to the pressure from the principal, forced a competition between the two to see which grade levels would have the highest achievement data and lowest student discipline. The principal likely meant well in her efforts as she led her assistant principals, yet the result was not a friendly competition. It led to what this assistant principal felt was more like two battleships at war, leaving her dreading her 2nd year in that position.

Another principal confidentially shared with us that one reason she is so thankful for having a Professional Learning Network (PLN) to turn to each day is because other administrators in her district are not supportive, willing to share ideas, or collaborate to benefit all schools. It is the conversations with people in her PLN that get her through the challenging days and help her gain new ideas to benefit her leadership and her building.

The question and dilemma lingers, is isolation created by the educational system? Or is it a byproduct of the nature of individuals? As we explore these concepts in this chapter, our hope is that it will become clearer. In addition, we delve into the potential pitfalls of isolation, and the impact on their leadership. Are you isolating yourself in your position? What steps can you take to keep yourself from feeling lost and alone in your building?

WHAT IS ISOLATION, AND HOW DOES IT IMPACT YOU?

At some point in our career, we have all felt isolated in our positions. The impact of this isolation may have impacted you to the point where you have become frustrated, transfer to a similar position in another school/district, or even to the extreme of wanting to leave your position. Although the story of the leader as isolated has become well known, the story of the actual isolation has been far overlooked.

As we planned to relate the story of isolation, we interviewed educators to understand their perceptions. The interviews of leaders throughout the country took place over the course of the last 3 years. We have interviewed school leaders at local, state, and national conferences, through Web 2.0 tools such as Skype and Google hangouts, and have read their blog posts on social media. Regardless of where they are in the country, large districts or small, affluent areas or low socio-economic areas, it seems that there is a common thread: Leadership is isolating! Throughout these informal interviews, there were many common themes:

- Education is not inherently a collaborative industry.
- School districts do not take enough time to encourage schools to work together.

- Educators are often hesitant to share for fear of criticism, or being labeled a "bragger."
- Once connected to social media, connected educators feel more isolated from their peers.
- There is no physical place to connect with people who are going through the same thing.
- Connected educators are faced with the reality that others view them as self-promoting, out to make others look bad, or wasting their time.

PROFESSIONAL LEARNING

Unfortunately, the learning to which most educators have become accustomed has been passive learning because that has been what they experienced in school. Schools have been organized in such a way that students were in rows and the teacher tended to be the sole proprietor of information. Students have been required to sit and behave in a passive manner in order to learn. On the same note, professional development has been organized in similar fashion with preplanned days of inservice or attending workshops, most of which are known by educators as "sit-and-get" or "drive-by PD." It is in these types of learning settings that educators feel as if they have no voice in what they need to learn, have to sit through something that doesn't even apply to them, or it is just another topic that "too shall pass" in the often transforming state of education.

The truth is that the vast majority of administrators were educated in passive learning schools. In keeping with the cycle of their understanding of learning, administrators have continued this process as they lead faculty meetings, workshops, and conferences. Even the graduate work required to become an administrator has been similar to what has existed in the American educational system for the past 200 years. Breaking this chain can be difficult, some would say, even impossible.

Thankfully, some aspects of professional learning, in just the past few years, has changed. In addition to workshops and traditional conferences, there are new innovations such as edcamps (labeled "un-conferences"), webinars, online discussions, as well as more inquiry-based conferences. To some, these new innovations offer a fresh perspective on education, and to others, it can lead to more feelings of isolation.

This progression of professional learning (from the "sit-and-get" to the hashtag) has many administrators shaking their heads in disbelief. For the majority of their life, they associated learning with sitting in a classroom with books, pens and pencils, and tests. Now, people are claiming to learn all the time, and on their phones! School districts are also faced with addressing this issue. Do they value time in the chair, or learning? How can a teacher that is learning on his or her own time/devices be given the same credence as those sitting in the chair for a certain amount of time?

PITFALLS

For starters, being a principal is mentally and physically tasking. Principals work long hours, are required to wear many hats, and deal with a range of stakeholders who all have a say in the direction of the school. We are required to be part of a system, and many struggle with the fact that "our" school is not "our" school. If we are in public schools, then we have a Board of Education, and Departments of Education at both state and federal levels that have a huge impact on our schools. In the private education world, principals have Boards of Trustees, diocese, parents who pay tuition, and other governing bodies and stakeholders to consider.

Principals are faced with many challenges that require a deeper understanding of the human condition. You never really understand the complexities of this until you're sitting at your desk and someone comes in and closes the door because he or she needs to "talk." These closed-door talks could range from needing to get out of work early for an appointment to classroom management struggles, questions about an observation, or even to cancer or the death of a family member. Life happens and teachers need the principal to be understanding and aware of their staff's situations. It is always amazing to see the unending list of responsibilities that are piled on educators outside of the school day. The relationships you build with your staff help in these situations, but they will not help in the overall isolation of the job. You may deal with Child Protective Services being called, deaths of parents or siblings of your students, legal issues, and so on. The biggest struggle in this part of the position is that the problems and situations are almost always confidential.

Emotional intelligence has been defined as the ability to recognize how leaders understand themselves and others (Goleman, Boyatzis, & McKee, 2005). Leaders have been prime candidates for stress, weight issues, and health issues. Using the concept of emotional intelligence, leaders utilize a process of renewal to deal with the sacrifices inherent in today's world of leadership. When leaders did not renew themselves, they ran the risk of becoming dissonant, and therefore, ineffective or burnt out (Boyatzis & McKee, 2005).

For a great deal of administrators, they rose to the position because they tended to volunteer for activities even when their plate was full. They generally had a tough time declining opportunities in the past because they felt that everything had the potential to obtain an advanced leadership position. Many administrators continue in their leadership position, taking full responsibility for all aspects of the school and taking initiative for many new aspects to improve their school culture/programs. The burden of this role can be daunting and taxing on any individual. In the process, many administrators become stressed out, and the volunteering becomes more detrimental to their well-being than the assumed benefit. When leaders are not in touch with their emotions, they can become dissonant, which leads to isolation.

Another pitfall that is common among administrators is nostalgia. Have you ever heard of the phrase "Nostalgia is the sign of a dying culture"? In terms of school administrators we say, "Nostalgia is the sign of an overwhelmed administrator." What does this mean? As new technologies and initiatives are created, it is difficult to keep up. During these times of change, many school administrators revert back to another time. This happens because they glamorize the past. They may feel that learning how to use e-mail was OK, so why would you need to understand Twitter or Google+? Yet the reality is, the time that they pine for was filled with just as many challenges as the present. Later in this book, as we describe the concept of mindset we will revisit this pitfall.

In a sense, as the pitfalls emerge, it is not that the connected leaders are more knowledgeable, but it is more a sense that they are better equipped, and we will share the tools to better equip your "toolbox" in the chapters to come. Pitfalls come and go. Pitfalls emerge with new regulations, new learning, and new positions, but connected leaders are better equipped to overcome them.

CONCLUSION

Isolation impacts educators, and as we have learned, school leaders. Some principals feel like they are on their own island with no one to connect with. As school leaders attempt to engage in professional learning through participating in traditional experiences such as graduate school, conferences, or meetings, they may feel further isolated. If this goes undetected or not addressed, the leader is prone to becoming dissonant and will experience difficulty with change. In the next few chapters, we will attempt to provide an alternative to the isolation in leadership and specific activities you can participate in to become more connected.

Reflection and Action

Reflection

By nature, leadership is an isolating position. However, there are many ways for you to become connected with others in your field to better equip yourself with a network to share ideas with, gain ideas from, and get support for yourself.

Reflect on your current situation and ask yourself:

- Who do I turn to as I reflect on myself as a leader?
- Who do I turn to for feedback on ideas or difficult situations?
- Do I have a variety of people to turn to discuss different types of issues or areas to gain ideas for?
- What resources do I currently utilize to continue my own professional learning and grow myself as a leader?

Action

Grab your favorite notebook (electronic or otherwise) and make a quick list of the people you identified as those you turn to in the reflection above.

- Are there any questions you have that they may not be able to answer?
- Are there any questions you wouldn't ask that set of people?
- Keep this list handy as you read Chapter 2. You'll be able to use these topics for some of your first tweets, or to discover new hashtags in discussion with your PLN.

Finding Your
Professional
Learning Network

"Twitter is the faculty room you always wanted."

—Adam Bellow

Educators and administrators that have become connected with others through social media have discovered a whole new world of learning at their fingertips. These connected educators call it "24/7 Professional Development (PD) when they want it," "PD from your couch," "learning at your fingertips," and "the staff lounge that never sleeps." As they build their Professional Learning Network (PLN) of people they are networked with online, they find it is very easy to learn about new educational practices that they didn't even know existed, because they were never seen in their building before and they never had a consultant come in and give them training on it. Yet, being connected allowed them to learn about those practices . . . for free!

Connected educators eagerly learn about new ideas they find on Twitter, Pinterest, or blogs, they share their professional and personal reflections on their own blogs, and they personally connect with other educators to have deeper conversations beyond 140 characters (via e-mail, Skype, Google Hangout, or even Voxer). Connected educators that make personal connections to those in their PLN have built a network of others that they know they can turn to for wisdom on specific subjects or even just to talk through an issue that they may be dealing with for the first time or simply want an opinion on how to handle it.

One of the tools that we use to connect with each other is Voxer. Voxer's website describes this service as a "Messaging, Walkie Talkie app for Team Communication." Theresa, Spike, and Jessica describe it as a lifeline. It seems a tad dramatic, but it truly is the best of all worlds. Voxer allows for individuals, and small or large groups, to have conversations and keep communication going. You can send messages and answer them when it is the best time for you. Theresa replies first thing in the morning or during a down moment in the office. Spike does most of his Voxer messaging during his commute. Jessica catches up on conversations while walking her dog. Voxer allows for any combination of voice messages, text messages, and photos. These groups have been used for book chats, continuation of Twitter chats, even

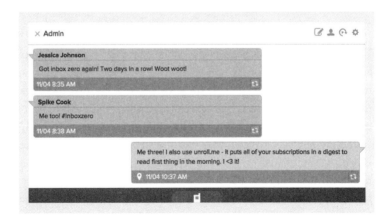

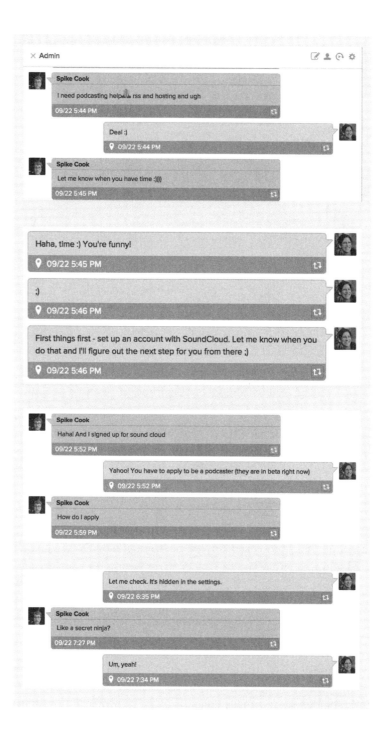

Spike Cook

I need podcasting help 🙏 rss and hosting and ugh

09/22 5:44 PM

Deal :)

📍 09/22 5:44 PM

Spike Cook

Let me know when you have time :))))

09/22 5:45 PM

Haha, time :) You're funny!

📍 09/22 5:45 PM

;)

📍 09/22 5:46 PM

First things first - set up an account with SoundCloud. Let me know when you do that and I'll figure out the next step for you from there ;)

📍 09/22 5:46 PM

Spike Cook

Haha! And I signed up for sound cloud

09/22 5:52 PM

Yahoo! You have to apply to be a podcaster (they are in beta right now)

📍 09/22 5:52 PM

Spike Cook

How do I apply

09/22 5:59 PM

Let me check. It's hidden in the settings.

📍 09/22 6:35 PM

Spike Cook

Like a secret ninja?

09/22 7:27 PM

Um, yeah!

📍 09/22 7:34 PM

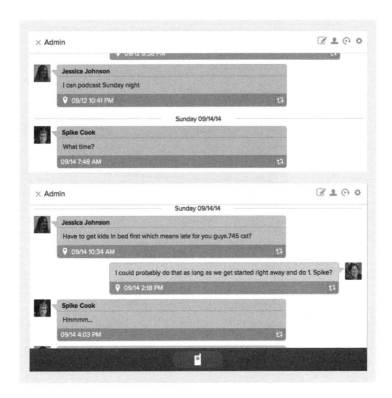

event planning. In fact, we have groups specifically for motivating each other, venting, and collaborating to write this book.

CONNECTION!

As a connected educator, you have already established a Twitter account. Your Twitter account includes a brief biography, a picture, and a link to either you or your school's website or your personal blog. We can't emphasize this enough. Chances are you have already begun to follow other people and you have some followers. So how do you become more connected? How can you use this tool to feel more connected?

Using hashtags to find great content or others that you may be interested in following will make things much easier (at the end of this chapter, we'll provide you with a list of people and hashtags we recommend you start following). Since the hashtag in Twitter is used to signify a special topic, group, or message, it is important to cull through it to find people with whom you feel comfortable. Then you start asking questions. What topic do you want to continue learning about? What are you dealing with in your job that needs improvement? What could use "fresh eyes" on?

If you have found a "match," then you will begin to have what you are looking for, and each time you come across a situation that warrants a new perspective, you can just ask your new Twitter friends (also known as "tweeps") from throughout the world. Also, anyone who is following you is going to see that you are seeking help or perspective, and they may join in on the conversation as well. Want the conversation to go beyond the 140 characters? Many connected educators are using Google Hangouts, Skype, Voxer, and even Edmodo to keep the conversation going. It may feel awkward at first, but very soon, you will benefit from starting the conversation in more ways than you can imagine.

TO BE PRIVATE OR PUBLIC?

Twitter allows you to set your account to be public or private. If your account is set to private, you must approve people to follow you; it is then similar to having "friends" on Facebook. If you tweet with a hashtag, others that are not following you will only see your tweet if your account is public. Users who have a profile set to private will not have their tweets shown in a hashtag search, which limits their ability to connect with others that they don't yet "know."

Jessica's Twitter account was set to private for nearly 2 years until the day she saw a great tweet from someone she followed and wanted to retweet it to share with others in her PLN, but the person's account was set to private, which won't allow you to retweet them. She realized that being private really limits your ability to expand your PLN. Jessica recalls that tweet having a powerful message and great content to share with others and realizing that if she retweeted it, the person would likely gain new followers for her PLN. In that moment, Jessica changed her account to public and has never had any regrets about doing so. Whether your account is public or private, you must always remember to practice digital citizenship and tweet responsibly.

Many Twitter newbies find themselves checking their Twitter stream as they "lurk and learn"; they don't feel comfortable tweeting or replying to anyone yet, but enjoy finding many "nuggets" in the tweets they read or find great resources as they check Twitter. Lurking and learning is great for continued learning, but it is a lot like checking Pinterest for ideas or reading an educational journal; it is a passive learning activity. Once educators begin contributing on Twitter by replying to others, participating in a Twitter chat, or tweeting ideas, then they will be seen by others as a connected educator and build their PLN. The next step is beginning to make personal connections to others on Twitter. This could be replying to someone's tweet to ask for more information, contacting someone that you notice has a great deal of expertise on a topic you are working on or even having extended conversations with someone from Twitter on the phone, on Voxer, Skype, or Google Hangout.

Why go beyond lurking and learning to make personal connections? Often when we talk with educators in our buildings or at conferences when we present, we find a common theme: Those that are on Twitter just following others, but not truly connecting with others to create a PLN, just don't get much out of Twitter and even make comments like "if I want to learn about something I can just Google it." Google has become such a necessity in our daily lives, but wouldn't it seem much more beneficial to talk to an actual person with experience and wisdom to offer on a subject then endlessly searching Google? A lot of the situations that administrators deal with go beyond what's appropriate to tweet about, yet to make the best decisions can do so better after talking it through with someone. Finding the best person for that situation is easy once you've connected with them and followed their tweets or participated in a chat with them. You will have a large group of people you can call on who are willing to help, and the conversations you've had or tweets you've followed will help guide which of those connections to contact in your time of stress. Administrators have unique positions and often cannot discuss these situations with anyone in their building due to the confidential nature, and may not feel comfortable discussing with their superintendent out of fear of not looking like they can do their job and may not even be comfortable talking to other principals in their district.

Here are a few sample tweets from the #principalpln crew:

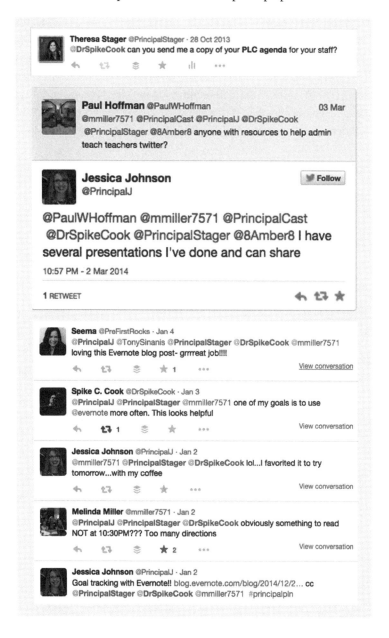

Connected educators have found it easier to talk to a removed peer, someone from their PLN with a like position in a district far away that can listen to a story without having any personal connections to the situation and offer feedback/support. It can be difficult to step out of a situation and look at it from all sides. Having someone disconnected who can listen to the facts without emotion or background can help you make an educated decision based purely on what is presented. That can be difficult if you are in the thick of the moment. They can also help diffuse and bring a little humor to the stress you are enduring. Despite having a team of colleagues with similar positions, connected teachers often use their PLN in the same way that administrators do.

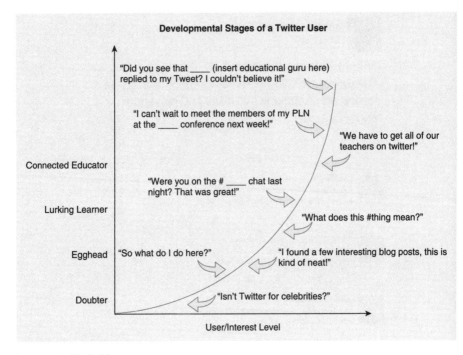

Developmental Stages of a Twitter User

"Did you see that ____ (insert educational guru here) replied to my Tweet? I couldn't believe it!"

"I can't wait to meet the members of my PLN at the ____ conference next week!"

"We have to get all of our teachers on twitter!"

Connected Educator

"Were you on the # ____ chat last night? That was great!"

Lurking Learner

"What does this #thing mean?"

Egghead   "So what do I do here?"   "I found a few interesting blog posts, this is kind of neat!"

Doubter   "Isn't Twitter for celebrities?"

User/Interest Level

Image created by J. Johnson

ESTABLISHING A PLN

Establishing a PLN is much more than just following others with similar roles/interests to see what they tweet about each day.

When Jessica presents to educators about Twitter, she emphasizes the importance of knowing who you are following and what they are passionate about so you can utilize their strengths. A large part of being a leader is not only knowing your strengths but embracing your weaknesses. No one wants to dwell on the things they struggle with or have a more difficult time with than others, but by knowing what your weaknesses are, you are one step closer to finding someone else who has a strength that is your weakness.

Jessica knows if she has a question about Response to Intervention (RtI), she can call on Curt Rees (@CurtRees) who is principal of a school that has been recognized by the Wisconsin Department of Public Instruction as being a "Model RtI School of Recognition." If she has a question about digital student portfolios or anything to do with literacy, she calls upon Matt Renwick (@ReadbyExample), a principal with solid literacy leadership and author of the book *Digital Portfolios*. When she led her school to implement a one-to-one iPad, program she contacted Jeff Gulan (@JGulan) numerous times since he was in his 3rd year of leading a one-to-one school, and she also followed the blogs and tweets from several other teachers that shared how they integrated iPads into their instruction. Who can she turn to when she needs more help, specifically with something that garners a great deal of trust?

When she was just having a bad day, Jessica knew she could use Voxer to talk to both Spike and Theresa, and even though they were both busy, they would hear her Voxer message and respond when they had time. For instance, Jessica suggested that the three read *The Mindful School Leader* (Brown & Olson, 2015), so that they could learn about how to deal with the stressors of school leadership. She sent the message through Voxer, and both Spike and Theresa agreed. As they read the book, they would discuss the concepts on Voxer, and encourage each other to exercise, meditate, and be present. *The Mindful School Leader* book, and ensuing discussion on Voxer helped us flush out sections of the book you are reading. This intertwined PD served us on many levels!

The three of us worked very hard to integrate the concepts discussed on the PrincipalPLN podcast into our daily life. For instance, when we did a podcast with Curt Rees on the concept of "e-mail inbox zero," we learned the importance of organization and time management. We realized we all struggled with critical leadership problems such as not being able to "turn off" work, struggling to leave work at an appropriate time, and responding to demands at all hours of the night (Brown & Olson, 2015).

In Jessica's example, she used several tools that allowed her access to overcome the pitfalls of leadership with her PLN. She used different aspects of her PLN to help her solve curriculum- and school-based problems, and used her Principal PLN cohosts to help address mindful issues. But before a leader can jump into the connected world, there are a few more things to conceptualize such as their comfort zone and mindset.

Early on in Spike's Twitter tenure, he received a Direct Message from Matt Renwick, a principal in Wisconsin. The message read, "They are saying bad things about you, click on this link." Since Spike knew Matt, he thought that someone had started a website where people were saying bad things about him. Of course he clicked the link, and when he did, he came across a message from his district that read, "This site is blocked due to security reasons." Spike panicked and called his superintendent, who then had the Informational Technology Supervisor investigate. They determined that the site was a phishing site designed by hackers in Russia. Spike then called Matt in Wisconsin to double check if he knew about the site. Matt changed his password and everyone was fine. Just like spam e-mail, Twitter is vulnerable to spam or phishing. We just advise that you not click on a link in a direct message from someone unless you know they're going to share a link with you. And never click on a link if it's associated with "Check out what people are saying about you" or "You won't believe this!"

Used with permission of Matt Renwick.

IT'S ABOUT BUILDING RELATIONSHIPS

What is common among connected educators is a growth mindset, a belief that their skills can continue to be developed through their commitment, passion for learning, and openness to take risks and try something new. An educator with a growth mindset checks social media (Twitter, Pinterest, Blogs, etc.) to see what kind of education conversations are taking place, tweets out a question to seek feedback, reflects on his or her practice through a blog or checks social media to see if there are new ideas he or she isn't even aware of yet. Connected educators are constantly seeking out ways to grow as a professional to benefit the learners in their classroom/school.

As was previously shared, many connected educators often go beyond Twitter to connect with others in their PLN. With each deeper interaction, they are building relationships with those in their PLN. You can identify the connected educators at a conference or workshop, because they often have Twitter up and ready to go at the beginning of the presentation. Theresa attended a workshop in which the presenter was already on Twitter and had created a hashtag for the presentation. She sent out a tweet that she was there and that the initial activity was going to send her social anxiety through the roof.

The presenter saw it during the activity, came over to reassure that it would be a great activity and not to worry, and introduced her to a few new faces in the crowd. She is still in contact with these new additions to her PLN and continues to share with them on a regular basis.

Used with permission of Stacey Shuh.

The fear in putting yourself out in any social situation is not being one of the "cool kids." It can be frightening! The great thing about Twitter is that we're all one of the "cool kids." Everyone is equal and everyone belongs, no matter your follower count or how long you've been online.

At the same conference, Theresa was looking for a place to sit for lunch. Someone yelled out "Principal Stager!" She had been recognized by her Twitter profile photo.

Used with permission of Joanna Van Raden.

STARTING YOUR OWN PLN

In the previous sections of this chapter, we reviewed the PLN and the importance of building relationships. As you explore these possibilities, you will find that there are many established PLNs, and many relationships already formed. To the newly connected educator, this can seem intimidating, like walking into high school as the new kid in the senior class. For instance, you may see a few educators constantly retweeting or commenting on each other's blogs, and then you may see them connect at a face-to-face conference. You must resist the urge to think that these folks are part of the "in-crowd" or that they may never have time for you. The reality is, these educators have built relationships with each other through common interests, online discussions, or even previous experiences. In this section, we will provide you with steps on starting your own PLN.

It has been stated numerous times that we only have 24 hours in a day. There is truly only so much time. How do you make the most of your time on social media, and direct your own learning beyond the established ways? Start your own PLN! Your PLN, however, can be made up of different people who are part of other PLNs. There are no exclusive memberships. The truth is that there are many people who want to connect with new people.

"Know thyself" is a cliché that is prevalent in many cultures. If you operate first knowing yourself, you will quickly be able to build your own PLN. As stated before, the twitter profile is your first step in presenting who you are to others. Want to be funny? Want to be serious? Want to be subject specific? It doesn't matter because you are merely describing you and someone will feel that you are a match for them.

When you seek out others, you will become adept in finding a range of people who inspire, match, challenge, and even share the same position as you. We suggest, especially when starting to build your own PLN, that you start small with about 5 or 10 people. Here are a few first steps:

- Follow 5 to 10 people on Twitter.
- Commit to reading their blog posts (usually if connected educators have a blog the link to it can be found in their Twitter bio).

- Participate in any weekly chats that they participate in. Some of you may be thinking that this is cyber-stalking, but the objective here is to determine if these educators are ones that share online about topics you want to learn and grow from.
- Respond to one of their tweets with a comment of appreciation or a question so you can learn more about what they are sharing.

Educator Spotlight—*Christopher Nesi*

Chris Nesi is a high school teacher from New Jersey, and he has inspired students and colleagues at the middle and high school levels. The passion Mr. Nesi has for education, technology, and learning are fueled by his PLN. Mr. Nesi is on the cutting edge of technology trends and how technology can be integrated into the classroom. He utilizes his personal blog and website, Twitter, and other social tools to continue is personal and professional growth. Mr. Nesi is creative, detail oriented, and tech-savvy with innovative ideas, energy, and the desire to get involved in his school community. Sharing what he learns with other educators and learning from other educators is what continuously shapes his own role as an educator.

Chris has always been a person who genuinely connects with people and connecting comes easy for him with his outgoing personality and friendly nature. Combine these traits with a desire to help others and you have a person who is great with people.

As a direct result of his PLN, Chris has developed and presented professional development workshops to teachers and collegiate faculty and personnel about a variety of education topics, including social media and connected learning for professionals and more recently sessions geared toward using the power of one's own voice for creating content rather than just curating the content of others. New technologies are becoming available every day and Chris enjoys expanding educators' understanding and use of these innovations for personal and professional use. Weekly, at his school, he conducts Wired Wednesdays where his colleagues meet for 15–20 minutes and quickly review an education topic or EdTech tool. These sessions allow people to get a conversation started and not overwhelm the participants.

Mr. Nesi is very active in the use and growth of his PLN, which has afforded him the opportunity to share his thoughts and perspectives with others via his contributions to Twitter chats and podcasts.

In 2014, Chris launched the *House of #EdTech* Podcast. Through his podcast, Chris explores how technology is changing the way teachers teach and the impact that technology is having in education. Whether you use it or not, technology is changing the way we teach and how our students learn. The podcast serves another tool for connecting with other like-minded educators, and Chris has built a valuable platform and community for people to continue their learning.

Tools like his podcast and a presence on Twitter have allowed Chris to create a limitless community for continued personal and professional growth. Chris is building his tribe through anytime, anywhere access to people with similar interests and passions. Chris is actively transforming himself from tech-savvy classroom teacher, who was always willing to troubleshoot for his colleagues, into a trusted and respected authority in education.

Chris's PLN provides a forum and support for his continued learning and connecting with people that bring value to him as both a professional and as an individual. The PLN is a key component of Chris' leadership skill-set acquisition. By building relationships with people, Chris connects with colleagues on a global scale, and these personal connections contribute to success with his peers.

Used with permission of Christopher Nesi.

CONCLUSION

We have found that establishing a PLN can be the most important factor in overcoming isolation in leadership. Many educators have reported that they feel the relationships they have established on Twitter are invaluable. If you cannot seem to find a PLN, we suggest that you start your own with like-minded educators with whom you feel a connection. We have provided a list to start with in the appendix of the book in case you need a springboard. In the next chapter, you will learn about the findings from our survey and how becoming connected brings with it a new set of challenges.

Reflection and Action

Reflection

In the first chapter, we discussed leadership isolation, and in the second chapter, we discussed the importance of becoming connected. As you reflect on these two aspects of leadership, we ask you to think about a few things:

- What do you see as a bigger challenge: isolation or developing a PLN?
- What kind of issues weigh on you mentally/emotionally that you wish you could discuss with someone?
- How do you feel Chris Nesi used his PLN to overcome isolation?

Action

- Go on Twitter and search the hashtag #principalpln. Pose a question about something that you would like to improve at your school or district. Within 24 hours, we guarantee that you will find at least one blog post, or other resource for you to use. Once the person gives you that information, set a time to discuss using Google Hangout or Skype. Invite anyone on the hashtag to participate.
- If you are really excited about becoming a connected administrator and want to jump in with both feet, join the Digital Leadership Challenge. You can find the MESPA challenge here: http://mespa .net/Digital_Leadership_Challenge_Driven_to_Collaborate.html

Maintaining Balance

"There's no such thing as work-life balance. There are work-life choices, and you make them, and they have consequences."

—Jack Welch

A typical morning for a connected educator includes checking Twitter to respond to any tweets mentioning them and then checking the Twitter stream for anything interesting, like following up on last night's #educoach chat or to see what other principals are tweeting with the #cpchat or #principalpln hashtag. While eating breakfast, he checks his Feedly account (a tool that keeps the newest blog posts of all the blogs that you subscribe to instead of having them clutter up your e-mail inbox or having to go to each individual site to check for new posts) and scans through several, spending time carefully reading a couple that appeal to his interest. He takes 5 seconds to tweet out a link to each blog post of interest, mentioning the blogger's Twitter handle, and adding a hashtag to the group he thinks will enjoy reading it too. He may even take a moment to add a personal comment to the author on the blog post. If it was a blog post that any of his teachers may benefit from, he goes another step further by e-mailing it to his teachers or adds it to his weekly memo for all staff to be able to read on Friday. Professional learning? Check. Professional collaboration with a Professional Learning Network (PLN)? Check. Learning leadership for his staff? Check. All in 15 minutes time before getting to work to start the day.

Getting connected and building a PLN does take additional time, but only the amount of time that you want to, and we have yet to meet a connected educator that regrets the time she spends for her ongoing learning through social media. In the example above, in 15 minutes, the connected educator accomplished so much for his professional learning. Something they read could have literally changed the teaching climate in their building. So why isn't everyone doing it? Why do some feel more isolated after spending that 15 minutes being inspired?

When we talk to connected educators about how being connected affects their relationships with their colleagues, we are finding that more and more connected educators are feeling a divide between themselves and their colleagues that are not connected, or even a feeling of isolation. But, how can one be connected, yet feel isolated? While an educator may be connected to hundreds or even thousands of educators across their state, country, or world, they feel isolated from the colleagues in their own building, because they are seen as "the crazy Twitter lady," "the social media guy," or "the bragging blogger." Educators on a whole are not people who "toot their own horn" or share accomplishments freely, so there are times that sharing information can be seen as boasting or arrogance. While connected educators are constantly sharing their reflections, ideas, and resources with one another, those that are not connected tend to see it as bragging and/or tend to keep their ideas to themselves, not sharing to benefit others.

Connected educators thrive from the ongoing learning and reflection that their PLN provides them with, but may become frustrated with their own colleagues in their schools who are not learning. We often find that those that won't even attempt to get connected also tend to be the type of educators that don't continue their professional learning unless it is mandated by their school/district. We often find that connected educators tend to have a growth mindset while those that continue to hear about the benefits of getting connected and choose not to (nor do they continue their professional learning in other ways), tend to have a fixed mindset (we'll further discuss mindset in Chapter 4). Thus, it is creating a divide between the educators that are continuous learners and those that believe they have learned everything. We have even found ourselves frustrated by other educators/administrators that do not continue their learning when we can see obvious answers/solutions, because of our PLN connections. Why would we get frustrated by someone else's lack of learning?

Anyone who has ever had the opportunity to have a discussion with other connected educators knows that their conversations in real life tend to be different from those of unconnected educators. It's almost like sitting in a group in which half of the people are talking about a TV show that they like to watch, and they get so excited talking about how they can't believe what happened or predict what they think will happen next; and the others in the group have never watched it so they have no way of taking part in the conversation. The people who don't watch the show have no way of joining in the discussion—unless it sounds interesting to them and they ask questions, like "What time is that show on?" "What channel is it on?" "Do I have to catch up on old episodes or can I just start watching next week?" Those having the conversation could also invite the *unwatchers* in: "Hey you should really check it out, and I know you'd like it!" But the conversation will continue to be divided unless that unwatcher tries watching the show. What's important to point out is that the unwatcher will likely never try watching the show without hearing the benefits of it or the encouragement from the watchers, much like the journey to get connected.

What makes connected conversations different than a discussion about last night's episode of *Walking Dead* or *The Big Bang Theory* is how powerful they can be, filled with great ideas, specific examples, schools to visit, articles to read, books to order, webinars to watch—all to help improve professional practice and student learning. Why wouldn't everyone want to be able to take part in that conversation?

We get frustrated when we see educators doing the same thing over and over and expecting different results, when an educator complains about something, but does nothing to try to improve the situation. We are disheartened when an administrator complains about how isolated her job is, because no one else in her building knows what she goes through on any given day and she has no one to talk to about her struggles.

An educator with a growth mindset, someone who wants to improve her craft, seeks out new resources and strategies to improve. She reflects and talks to others to get feedback and ideas to help her improve her practice. She is comfortable exploring an array of learning opportunities from books and articles to conversation and connection to continue her learning. She attends conferences, meetings, and workshops as funding allows. A connected educator can do all of these things to continue her professional learning, but with the touch of a phone/tablet at any time that is convenient for her, she expands her connections beyond the colleagues in her building.

WHAT CONNECTED ADMINISTRATORS HAVE TO SAY

During the research phase for this book, we reached out to our PLN through a survey. In order to promote the survey, we used Facebook, Twitter, and Google+. We also encouraged our listeners on the PrincipalPLN podcast to take the survey. The survey was open for feedback for 2 months. There were 48 respondents. We asked the following questions:

- In what ways are you connected to other administrators?
- What benefits do you receive from being connected to other leaders?

- What drawbacks have you encountered?
- Do you have any additional comments that you would like to share?

Respondents were able to choose multiple answers from the options that followed, or add their own. When we analyzed the data, there were a few points that confirmed what we originally thought, and there were a few surprises. For instance, in Figure 3.1, we were not surprised that 100% of the self-identified connected educators responded that they use Twitter. We were surprised, and discussed with each other, that Facebook was only used by 40% of respondents to connect with other administrators. In the discussion, Spike and Theresa said that they connect with other administrators using Facebook, but Jessica uses Facebook exclusively for family, friends, and her staff members that add her. Spike and Theresa also use Facebook to connect with their faculty and staff because, as Theresa said, "I can learn about the life events of my staff which leads to better conversations while at school."

The data reported in Figure 3.2 confirmed that administrators are using social media to gain new ideas for themselves and their teachers. We

FIGURE 3.1   In what ways are you connected to other administrators? (N = 48)

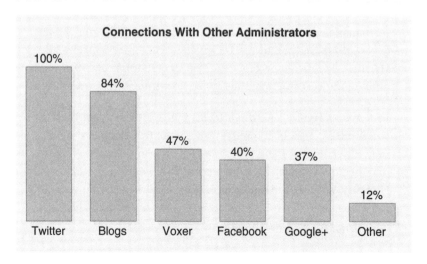

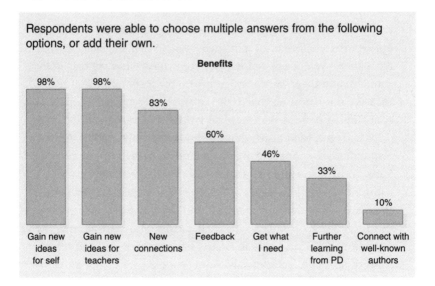

FIGURE 3.2 What benefits do you receive from being connected to other leaders? (N = 48)

Respondents were able to choose multiple answers from the following options, or add their own.

Benefits

98%	98%	83%	60%	46%	33%	10%
Gain new ideas for self	Gain new ideas for teachers	New connections	Feedback	Get what I need	Further learning from PD	Connect with well-known authors

were surprised that only 33% use it to further learn from conferences. As we discussed this figure, each of us have used social media to further discussions from local, state, and national conferences. Twitter allows attendees to have a backchannel discussion during a conference using the conference hashtag and allow non-attendees to "see" what they're learning at the conference. Spike told the story of hanging out with Ned Kirsch (@betavt) and Katrina Stevens (@katrinastevens1) at the ASCD Conference in Philadelphia in 2012. He still remains connected with Ned and Katrina, and they will often send tweets to each other to see how things are going.

In terms of Figure 3.3, which focused primarily on drawbacks of social media, 58% of the respondents identified that they feel like they never stop working as a drawback to being connected. As we discussed these results, we all agreed that this is our biggest drawback. Honestly, if you asked our spouses, they would agree that we work too much. Yet, each of us look at the "work" of being connected as enjoyable and well worth our time.

FIGURE 3.3   What drawbacks have you encountered due to being connected? (N = 48)

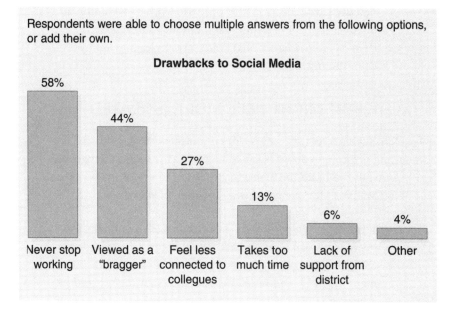

Respondents were able to choose multiple answers from the following options, or add their own.

Drawbacks to Social Media

58%	44%	27%	13%	6%	4%
Never stop working	Viewed as a "bragger"	Feel less connected to collegues	Takes too much time	Lack of support from district	Other

Those that selected the response of feeling like they never stop working in our survey also made the following comments expressing the benefits, despite the time:

- "The positives of being a connected educator/leader, far outweigh the negatives. It does take time, but I am so motivated by my colleagues' ideas (both near and far)."
- "I have benefited so much from becoming a connected educator, because I have been able to hear what others are doing and discover topics for further exploration. Additionally, I have been able to share things with my colleagues and adapt things to my situation."
- "It does take time, but the result of being connected is that I feel like I am driving my own PL (professional learning) and can help others access their own as well. We can be very focused."

- "Being connected challenges me in my daily actions and thoughts."
- "I have benefited so much from becoming a connected educator, because I have been able to hear what others are doing and discover topics for further exploration. Additionally, I have been able to share things with my colleagues and adopt things to my situation."

WHY YOU MIGHT FEEL MORE ISOLATED

In our survey responses, we also found comments that confirmed our feeling of isolation about being connected. As we went through the comments, we heard the theme that drove us to write this book. In a sense, we have all experienced what the respondents shared with us.

- "I wanted to blog about my internship, and my principal told me that it wasn't appropriate. The inability of my leaders to recognize the power of social media made it very difficult for me to really be connected because they continually told me it was not appropriate."
- "It's been a struggle to get others in district connected and to see the benefits. They view it as getting info or bragging, not as a PL (personal learning) tool. Balancing the act now of how to help others grow PLN without making it 'something else for them to do' where they miss the benefits."
- "I feel my growth is so much greater outside the building than in it, and find challenges bringing amazing learning in house to non-connected colleagues who have yet to embrace the growth mindset that being connected leads to through reflection and collaboration."

These quotes have been reverberating throughout the experiences of connected educators near and far. It really is a conundrum that plagues the connected educator. The more connected you become, the more isolated you feel. This is happening to connected educators on a daily basis as they try to share their newly discovered knowledge with colleagues. They are also experiencing this isolation as they go on interviews for prospective jobs. In addition to isolation, this harsh reality leads to frustration, despair, and many reconsider their path. Since we know that we are alone, it is always good to hear from someone who is willing to share their story.

Educator Spotlight—*Shawna Miller*

Shawna Miller is the Director of Professional Learning in Lewisville Independent School District in Texas. She came into this role after taking the lead as elementary school principal on transforming her school; it's learning spaces, moving to inquiry learning, technology integration, using student voice, and so on. Since her students' school experiences were drastically different from what parents were used to, Shawna found herself needing to share information with parents, because they weren't sending home worksheets anymore. She first found Twitter to be a great way to share what her school was doing.

Transforming schools had been a district focus that Shawna took to heart and ran with in her school. When she shared with others in the district, she found many in disbelief that what she was doing was actually possible. Looking to connect with others that were doing the same kind of work, Shawna's Twitter use evolved into being about her personal learning, discussing experiences with others, and possibly visiting their schools. As a result, her learning exploded through connections with blogs, webinars, and edcamps. Being connected is what fuels Shawna's fire. As her connected experience evolved, she realized that being connected is all about learning, not just sharing your school's story.

One of Shawna's frustrations when talking with administrator colleagues was when she talked about being connected. When she shared about how she uses Twitter and what she gains from it, some common responses to her included "Yes, but all people do on Twitter is brag," or "I have no idea how you find time to tweet, I have lots of important work to do." Shawna was doing important work, and Twitter helped her do it even better. Shawna sees herself as being a Lead Learner, and Twitter provides her with the opportunity to continue her learning from others. To her, being a connected educator is not something you do, it is who you are. Thanks to her Twitter PLN, she is not alone, she connects with others that understand where she's at and challenge her to extend her comfort zone.

In her new role as Director of Professional Learning, Shawna's current priority is trying to shift the mindset of leaders, teachers, and administrators, toward becoming lead learners themselves. She has been finding a common trend with the administrators she works with: It is easy for the unconnected educators to get bogged down in the daily "ins and outs" of "doing school" that has little impact on student learning. When you are going to transform education, your personal learning is a must, and the connectedness and daily focus on learning impacts what you do each day. So how can she change that focus in administrators? Two areas she's noticed about those that are hesitant to get connected include the following: (1) They struggle to see the benefits (fixed vs. growth mindset) and (2) say they don't have time. They don't realize that the time is for learning and that they need to make learning a priority so their decisions and actions impact student learning and success. Shawna is currently focusing on helping them to see the benefits of being connected and learning, that they would be working smarter and not just harder.

Used with permission of Shawna Miller.

BECOMING THE LINCHPIN

Want be able to have the best of both worlds? We recommend that you recognize the struggles and obstacles associated with isolation both as a connected educator and someone who is unconnected. Set a goal for yourself to be a linchpin. Linchpins, according to Seth Godin, are the indispensable members of the organization who cannot be replaced because they have become too valuable. Yes, that's right, we want you to be the indispensable connected educator that helps the unconnected see the value of being connected. Sounds easy, right?

More and more conferences these days are including sessions on getting connected. If one of the conferences that you attend each year hasn't had such a session, then submit a proposal and lead it yourself. Back in 2011, when Jessica finally ripped off the "private" Band-Aid to go public with Twitter and began truly expanding her PLN, she made it her personal mission to spread the word about Twitter, because each new person she could get connected on Twitter was another person she could learn from. She was surprised by how few administrators in Wisconsin she could find on Twitter. In fact, she only found one: Curt Rees. She sought him out on Twitter (they had never previously met), and they used the power of social media and Google tools (Google Docs, Google Presentation, and Skype—Google Hangout hadn't been created yet) to plan their first presentation for their state administrators conferences.

Jessica created an open Google document for Wisconsin Educators on Twitter, which has now grown to list over 300. Over the years, they have presented several times, and expanded their presentation to include other Wisconsin administrators, Jay Posick and Matt Renwick. In 2014, they joined forces with several other administrators and educators (through Twitter connections that have extended to further conversations on Voxer) to plan and run "social media lounges" at a variety of conferences (state administrators conference, state technology conference, state reading association) throughout the year with the goal of supporting others to get connected on tools of their interest: Twitter, Voxer, Blogging, Pinterest, and so forth.

You don't have to "Go Big" with sharing the power of being connected. Start small with your own staff. Take some time in a staff meeting to show staff how being connected has impacted your learning and show them a few hashtags they may be interested in, like a specific grade level or state chat. Find out how many of your staff are already connected and maybe didn't share it before. Start a bulletin board in the staff lounge for staff to add their Twitter handles to. Take some time to find tweets, pins, and blog posts that your teachers might benefit from and add them to your weekly memo. Suggest Twitter users to follow. Provide a hashtag you think they could benefit from. This allows you to model being connected and share great resources while not pushing or having your staff feel overwhelmed by this new medium.

CONCLUSION

Our survey results both confirmed the basis for this book and our own feelings about connection, isolation, and leadership. We were able to listen to our PLN about what issues they were specifically having once connected. It certainly wasn't the panacea we had always hoped. We know from this experience, that becoming connected is valuable, and we wouldn't trade it for the world. As linchpins in our organizations, we attempt to help both the connected and unconnected. This is certainly not an easy task either. We know that change takes time, and that will be addressed in the next chapter.

Reflection and Action

Reflection

In this chapter, Shawna Miller talks about the downside of being connected such as others not wanting to join her. Think about these questions as you reflect on the process of becoming connected in order to combat isolation.

* How would you respond to your colleague when they tell you they have no time to read a book or a blog on social media?
* How would you support someone like Shawna in your district?
* How would you compare Chris's experience with Shawna's?

Action

Everyone who becomes connected and sees the possibilities of social media wants to tell the whole world. They can get disappointed when not everyone jumps at the excitement. Not only that, but there are some people who may actually be working against you. Yikes. Getting buy-in can be a difficult road.

We suggest that you get started helping others get connected by following a set of methods we have found successful:

1. Be open and transparent: Once you become connected, be sure to share it with your colleagues, and do not hold this gift to yourself.

2. Establish norms: What does it look like? What does it sound like? When can people access, and more importantly, why?

3. Build capacity: Assist those who will be trying social media for the first time. It can be intimidating, and people need support.

4. Celebrate early successes: Be sure to celebrate when someone sends their first tweet, or finds their first resource on Pinterest. Jessica likes to celebrate by announcing a Twitter newbie by tweeting out a welcome to them (including their Twitter handle) and includes the appropriate hashtag for what group of teachers will likely help that teacher become connected.

5. Do not mandate: Some people will just never buy in, and that is OK, people will resent you if you make them participate in social media. Jessica has some teachers that are not comfortable with social

media, but will ask her, "Could you tweet out to find ideas about _____ for our grade level?"

6. Get out of the way: Once a bunch of people have bought in, then you can step to the side and let them run with it!

7. Let teachers lead: Once you see others being connected, give them the opportunity to share with others. Ask them to lead sessions on how they are using social media tools for their professional learning and to help their colleagues.

8. Set a date to share: Maybe it is a faculty meeting or an informal after-school meeting. Send invites, e-mails, and follow up. After you've shared, be sure to send a message to your PLN to let them know how it went.

CHAPTER
4

Embracing Isolation
and Connection
With Mindset

*"The view you adopt for yourself profoundly affects the way
you lead your life."*

—Carol S. Dweck,
Mindset: The New Psychology of Success

Is it possible that we can be both isolated and connected at work
and online using social media? In this chapter, we explain how
through the concept of mindset you may feel isolated and connected at the same time. We all tend to gravitate to those who are
similar to us. It could be common interests or views on the world,
but there are some people that we just click with. On the other
hand, we are often faced with other people who we can't seem to

agree with, no matter the situation. This all could be based on our mindset.

WHAT IS MINDSET?

Are leaders born or made? Are some people natural leaders or do they need to work on it? Can leaders change? These are the age-old questions that people have been debating for centuries. There are usually two camps: leaders are born leaders, or leaders are made. Those who possess a growth mindset seek to grow and learn from experiences, and in contrast, those with a fixed mindset tend to view their learning based on their intelligence.

For instance, think of the aspiring school leader. Many are seen as brilliant and are treated as such. They can interview well, and shine as they come up through the ranks. Yet they end up struggling when they are in an actual leadership position. Why do these leaders, when faced with challenges, struggle? Chances are if leadership came easy to them, they didn't work on it. They may be suffering from a fixed mindset. Some people are so caught up on failure, losing, making mistakes. It's a shame because by struggling in their profession and leadership experiences, they are truly missing out on life's lessons. We can blame educators, politicians, parents, teacher, and bureaucrats, but not for long, though. We see a tide is slowly turning where people are beginning to see that the innovative mindset can no longer be burdened by an educational system that is, at its core, based on standardized tests, developmental appropriateness, and educators who are hyperfocused on good/bad.

So how does this play out in school? We need to praise the *process*, not the *product*. For instance, if a student shows success on a math assessment the appropriate feedback to help them avoid developing a fixed mindset would be "You must have worked really hard for that or you are putting in a lot of effort" as opposed to saying, "You are so smart at math!" If you praise the process, you will be creating a lifelong learner, and someone who values growth. This is no different for school leaders. How are you going to change the conversation and show what you and your school community value?

Jessica talks about what she calls "leading her teachers with a coaching hat," because she gets into classrooms often to observe and provide them with nonevaluative feedback. It took years of constantly telling her staff that she is giving feedback to help improve for many to realize that she's not always evaluating them with each "dose" of feedback and believes that this is what helps contribute to developing a culture of growth mindset in her staff.

Educators, with some exceptions, are lifelong learners. They are constantly seeking to grow and understand their learners each year. This is not easy, but with the help of their peers, administrators, researchers, and other practitioners the system is set up to keep improving. For instance, we use observation preconferences with teachers to ask them what they want us to look for to provide specific feedback on so they can improve. We put the desire for growth in their hands here, even though the evaluation obligations are on us. At the elementary level that could mean a whole host of subjects or specific concepts, such as how many higher level questions are asked, if the teacher calls on more boys than girls, or the specificity of the teacher's feedback.

The trust that we build together allows them the opportunity to attempt to improve in an area. Quite often they perform better and, at the postconference, have much more of a critique on themselves, especially if they are of the growth mindset and are focused on improvement. For summative evaluations the administrator can continue to cultivate a growth mindset by asking teachers to come to the summative meeting with their own summative ratings and let the teachers start the discussion with their reflection of their self-evaluation. While the summative evaluation must be completed by the administrator, the discussion focus can still be focused on what the teacher knows/reflects on and wants to improve on professionally. More often than not, the teacher and administrator are on the same page and again, those with a growth mindset are often "harder" on themselves than the administrator.

Until the publication of Carol Dweck's *Mindset*, all of this was just a debate. Carol Dweck's research has illuminated this paradigm as growth or fixed mindset. Ask yourself these questions: Do you get to a certain part of your career, and decide that you have learned everything? Do you continue to push yourself and grow? This can impact you and your profession as you seek to find others to learn from.

ISOLATED BY PRINCIPLE

Have you ever been to a staff meeting and, even though you are sitting with colleagues, felt isolated from everyone in the room? Have you ever been working in a small group with other colleagues and felt isolated because of the ideas being shared? We call this being isolated by principle, and it could be detrimental to your progress—if you let it!

The more that we have been learning about and discussing isolation, the more we realize it is a common feeling among everybody, not just administrators. Well-known author and speaker (many have seen her on Oprah) Brene Brown writes about isolation in her book *Daring Greatly* (2012). Brown writes about how feeling disconnected can be a normal part of life, despite the many connections we have on Facebook or other forms of social media. She shares that one step beyond disconnection is isolation. Brown cites authors Baker and Stiver:

> We believe that the most terrifying and destructive feeling that a person can experience is psychological isolation. This is not the same as being alone. It is a feeling that one is locked out of the possibility of human connection and of being powerless to change the situation. In the extreme, psychological isolation can lead to a sense of hopelessness and desperation. People will do almost anything to escape this combination of condemned isolation and powerlessness. (p. 140)

We call this isolation by principle, because even though you are not the only human being in your building, even though you are not the only administrator in your district, you are bound to feel isolated. This occurs when a principal sees what changes in instruction need to happen in his school building, yet is only getting resistance from teachers. When a teacher leader is trying to use new online tech tools in her classroom that she has learned about from others online, the tech director will not unblock the websites, she feels isolated. Theresa created the first classroom blog in her high school classroom when she began teaching. Every site she created was blocked because of the interaction the students could have with each other, and she was told this would not change. When a district administrative meeting focuses its time discussing issues that do not pertain to you or with which you fundamentally disagree, you feel frustrated and want to find someone who will listen to what you just had to sit through. These are all common examples of what we call isolation by principle, and we're certain you can think of five additional examples in the next minute.

In preparing for the book, Spike shared with Theresa and Jessica about a previous job experience where he was isolated by principles. In a meeting, Spike expressed concerns about consistency with student discipline in the school. He raised the concerns with the best intentions, but it was not received the same way from everyone involved. Even before the meeting ended, Spike began to feel very isolated from his colleagues. He learned a valuable lesson. Sometimes people can become very defensive when challenged on their beliefs/principles, which can lead to feelings of isolation. This is especially true when the majority of an organization hold the same principles to be true and they become engaged in *groupthink* (Whyte, 1952).

Ironically, groupthink is also emerging in the connected world of social media, but what happens to you when you feel that members of your Professional Learning Network (PLN) are excelling and you are not? This is an often overlooked aspect to being isolated even though you are connected. We talked with a principal, who chose to remain anonymous, and she shared her frustrations. "Once I established my PLN, I felt like I was really part of a group moving education forward. Then I noticed that certain individuals were gaining in followers, presenting at conferences, and getting book deals. I began to wonder what was wrong with me. Why wasn't I getting picked?

What happened to my seat at the cool kids table?" As the principal expanded on her isolation, she concluded, "Eventually I had to get over it. I was hurt because I thought we were all on the same team. Some people are in it for themselves. I ended up connecting with other educators, and I feel much less isolated."

Another way that connected educators feel isolated from their PLN is from positivity. One of the guiding principles of connected educators is to use the platform to positively promote their school, classroom, or ideas. This unwritten code has both positive and negative consequences. By keeping it positive, educators avoid getting in trouble with their local community. On the flip side, other connected educators read the endless positive blogs, comments, and tweets wondering if anyone ever has a bad day or questions their purpose. Deep down you know that these educators *must* have something they want to vent about. Educators also know that their lives become public as soon as they accept their first position, so venting over social media could impact their professional reputation. Connected educators who have a bad day, and usually turn to their PLN for support, may need to do so via backchannels discussed earlier or not vent their frustrations at all.

CONNECTED BY PRINCIPLE

In the reverse of the previous section, have you felt synergy when working with other staff members on a project? Do you find yourself gravitating to certain individuals in meetings or projects because you know that things will get completed without drama, arguing, or fighting? We call this being connected by principles.

Motivational speaker Jim Rohn is well known for saying, "We are the average of the five people we spend the most time with." People with a growth mindset seek out connections that will help them to continue to grow as individuals and human beings. We often gravitate toward people that we want to be more like or that have the same attitudes and interests as we do. When we expand our PLN to include great educators, we are trying to improve the average of the five people we spend the most time with. One of the Voxer groups that Jessica is a part of includes several authors, speakers, principals of schools that have received state and national recognition, and principals recognized as Principal of the Year for their state. Each day that she listens in to the conversations, whether personal or professional in nature, she feels as if she grows from just hearing their stories and hopes she can become "average" of these five amazing leaders.

In further exploring your principles, you may find yourself gravitating to those who you seek to emulate. Social media makes this easier than simply sitting next to your best work friend in a meeting. We often connect with those on social media whom we want to be like. For instance, when Spike was researching topics for his first book, he intentionally followed educational authors on Twitter. He wanted to understand their writing process, and would often tweet them a question or a thought. In return, some authors were able to give him feedback, or suggestions. One author, in particular, was the principal/author Peter Dewitt. Spike would send Peter blog posts to read. Peter kept encouraging Spike to write about the innovations occurring at his school. Both Peter and Spike were connected by their principle, and it just so happened that they eventually met at the National Association for Elementary School Principals annual conference. They shared a similar view on the impact of digital leadership in the 21st century.

Most people report that finding and maintaining a PLN in social media is the easy part. As you cull through the various chats and discussions, you end up, as stated before, finding synergy. Week after week, blog post after blog post, everyone says similar things no matter the topic. It feels great to have this group, right? The downside to this activity is that, as Spike shared in the last section, is the emergence of groupthink (Whyte, 1952).

For those of us that are already connected with an established PLN, we need to be mindful of how we present ourselves to those that are not connected, so we do not create a divide or further isolate ourselves from one another. You may be asking yourself, "Why would I create a divide?" The truth is, it is easy to do this without realizing. Any connected educator that has gone to a conference with excitement about meeting their "tweeps" (people they are connected to on Twitter) is likely to isolate themselves from others without even realizing it. They pass by others that they do not know, yet run excitedly to hug people they recognize from Twitter and start conversations immediately as if they have been friends from kindergarten. We need to remember that for those not yet connected, or just getting started, we may be creating an image of "members only," preventing others from joining in our conversation or even further perpetuating our own "groupthink."

Educator Spotlight—*Jay Posick*

Jay Posick is the principal at Merton Intermediate School, a fifth- to eighth-grade school in Merton, Wisconsin. Jay has been a middle school person for nearly 25 years as a teacher for 12 years in seventh and eighth grades, an assistant principal for 5 years, and in his current role as principal for 7 years. Merton Intermediate School is a one-to-one Chromebook and BYOD (Bring Your Own Device) school using Google Apps for Education as well as a variety of other online tools. The heart of the school, however, is the students and staff who receive incredible support from the families in Merton.

Jay began his Twitter journey in 2010 when a teacher, Chris Reuter (@chris_reuter), who is now the principal at Franklin Middle School, held a Twitter Tuesday discussion before school. Jay admits he was a bit leery of this new way of learning, but the information Chris shared and the constant flow of information and ideas was exciting. Jay quickly became addicted, mostly lurking and retweeting, and now the PLN Jay has developed has helped him stretch his thinking and the thinking of those around him.

Jay has found a number of ways to try to help the teachers in Merton connect with others around the world.

1. Jay has continued with Twitter Tuesdays once a quarter, meeting before school in the library with anyone who is interested. Sometimes, it's a group of teachers, and sometimes it's just one, but sharing the value of Twitter with them has increased the number of staff who are becoming more connected.

2. The Building Leadership Team did a Google hangout with Adam Welcome (@awelcome), the principal of John Swett Elementary School in California

(@jseroadrunners), and two of his teachers to help explain the benefit of Twitter to connect his teachers to one another within their school. They are able to share stories and ideas with one another without needing formal meetings. This is our next step in getting our staff connected using social media.

3. Jay has a section of his weekly nuts and bolts called "Tweets, blogs, and quotes" that provides information of what he has found as he connects with others on Twitter and Voxer. Here is an example at http://bit.ly/1CeQCyh.

4. Jay has hosted Twitter chats using the hashtag #mertonint. The first one was attended by seven students, one parent, and one teacher—a great start! Before the chat, Jay and the students did a Twitter 101 session in order to provide some assistance. The second chat was a joint venture with Ted Huff (@TedHiff—yes, his username is not spelled the same as his "real name") and his middle school in Missouri (@FHMchat—Francis Howell Middle School). Ted and Jay are both trying hard to spread the word about Twitter in their school communities.

Every school day, Jay attempts to post what's happening in Merton on the school's Twitter account (@mertonint). There are pictures, reminders, links to daily school announcements, and links to his weekly newsletter (https://www.smore.com/re5zu). There is a link on the school's webpage to Twitter and the sign in front of the school always has the line "Follow @mertonint."

With all of the access staff and families have to Twitter, Jay is still frustrated by the overall lack of excitement about what Twitter can offer staff and families. He is currently trying to involve more staff in social media so that they can connect with others who are like or, more importantly, unlike them. Following only those who agree with you doesn't help you grow as an educator or a person. It is important to be stretched and questioned in order to learn. We don't get any better just hearing others tell how what we're doing is awesome. We need pushback to get better.

Used with permission of Jay Posick.

CONCLUSION

What is your mindset? After reading this chapter, can you move toward finding others with the same principles no matter if you are in your organization or connecting on social media? Is connection a mindset? Is isolation a mindset? These are the questions that are designed to keep you grounded in the why. We all know it is easier to work with certain people than others, but will you let it isolate you, or will you let it connect?

For school leaders avoiding the pitfalls that come along with isolation and connection are real. We know it is difficult to be the person in the organization who is eager to learn, excited to try new things, only to be criticized and celebrated all at the same time. This paradox that we face can be liberating and frustrating! Yet we firmly believe that the work to push education and learning to a new paradigm rests on the shoulders of those who have a growth mindset and are ready to take a chance.

Reflection and Action

Reflection

In this chapter, we wanted to make sure that everyone realizes that by becoming connected your world will not necessarily change overnight. Here are a few questions for reflection.

- Do I have a growth mindset, a mindset in which I believe I can continue to learn and grow?
- How will I devote the time it takes to build a PLN and become connected?
- How will I avoid groupthink in my organization and social media?

Action

- Read *Mindset* by Carol Dweck and then be prepared to share it with the teachers in your building.
- Find a colleague that shares a different mindset than you. Agree to work on a collaborative project. Use this experience to grow and learn about their mindset.
- Participate in a Twitter Chat (http://cybraryman.com/chats.html) and provide a different perspective. See how others react to a different point of view.
- Continue to stay connected to the colleagues in your vicinity, while sharing the great things you learn from those you are connected to online.

CHAPTER
5

Now What? So What? What's Next?

"Solitude is pleasant, loneliness is not."

—Anna Neagle

Throughout this book, we have brought you through the progression of isolation to connection to isolation back to connection. This process is cyclical. You start out feeling isolated, and then you use social media to connect yourself to a broader audience, and you feel isolated from your colleagues. You work on getting more buy-in and building capacity with your colleagues, and you feel more isolated from your online Professional Learning Community (PLN). You place more emphasis on developing your PLN and you realize how long it takes to grow. It is quite a ride being a connected educator!

NOW WHAT? SO WHAT?

We know that leadership positions are isolating by the nature of their role and that the multitude of responsibilities we bear can be daunting and possibly lead to burnout. We know that building connections to others in similar positions to build our own PLNs helps us to learn and grow and receive much needed assistance on difficult situations that we encounter in our roles. We can have the kind of conversations that we just can't have with colleagues in our building, the conversations that truly help us to survive the island that we work on so we can keep on moving forward.

We can become known by our colleagues as the "crazy Twitter guy" if we're not careful with how we message our excitement for our online learning or we can become known as the "social media guru" that our colleagues turn to as they decide to jump on the bandwagon of online learning. We can cram social media down our teachers' throats and force them all to get connected, or we can choose wisely what resources to share in ways that they will see the benefits while learning new tools/strategies to benefit the learners in their classrooms.

We know that if we open ourselves up to be more transparent and vulnerable with some of our tweets and blogs that we can receive some invaluable feedback from others in similar positions to help us with our professional journey. Yet, if we're not careful, we can open ourselves up too much and encounter backlash that can mess with our confidence levels, or worse, create bigger waves with our superintendents, school board members, or community members (this is more rare). We also recognize that if we become too connected, we can miss out on the opportunities to build relationships with the colleagues in our buildings or let precious life experiences with our family and friends pass right before our eyes if we don't look up from our devices.

So, just like anything else in our personal and work lives, we try to find a perfect balance that works for each of us. Or better yet, since there really is no way to perfectly balance everything on our plates, we try to counterbalance by choosing the ways and times for us to be connected to our PLN and pulling back when we need to turn the devices off. For one person, this may mean checking Twitter and blogs every morning and during a lunch break. For another, it may mean checking the feed only in the evening after the kids are in bed; for someone else, it may be during scheduled Twitter chats each week with groups that are always of interest. Taking it to the next level, these may include actual discussions in individual and group conversations on Voxer. Or it may be a combination of all of the above, in whatever manner works best for that individual. In any way, it helps the professional to connect with others to survive the isolation, yet remain connected to those in their buildings to avoid becoming divided from the unconnected.

HOW CAN YOUR NEW LEARNING HELP YOU GROW AS A LEADER?

Avoiding isolation as a leader, as stated before, is inevitable. However, you control the extent to which isolation will have an impact on your leadership and for how long. We all go through periods when we are juggling the responsibilities of being a leader. There is an ebb and flow to the process, and it is critical to use this new information to help you grow.

One of the clichés about leadership is the life cycle of the butterfly. As aspiring leaders, we are in our cocoon preparing ourselves in graduate school and internship hours for the leadership opportunity. Then we get our first administrative position and voila, we become butterflies, and we can apply all of the information we stored away in our cocoon. Unfortunately, based on this analogy, we would never need to learn anything new. Many leaders feel this way, and it is a trap. In all honesty, we go through many cycles as a butterfly.

Growth and development in leadership is at the cornerstone of isolation and connection. Learning new things can be a challenge, and applying the learning can be difficult. Leaders must be able to take risks and be comfortable with failure. For instance, when you become connected and develop a sustainable PLN, you are taking a risk. You are opening yourself up to a new world full of connections and learning, while at the same time potential ridicule and criticism. What a conundrum! Both experiences can teach you important lessons—about you!

In order to combat isolation from your PLN or your colleagues, it is important, as stated previously, to be the linchpin. How you model transparency, how you connect your learning, and apply it will assist you greatly in the growth of leadership. Sometimes we need to just "get things done" and not worry what others may think or how they may criticize. Often times, it says more about them (their criticism) than it does about us. It is real, and it can pull you down or pull you out. We all agree that you cannot let it. You have too much to offer. You have so much more opportunity to grow.

WHAT'S NEXT FOR YOU?

If we have done our job with this book, we have given you much to think about. As you go through the next few months of your leadership, pay particular attention to your mindset: Is it fixed or growth minded? How will you combat isolation that comes with working with others in either social media or in your organization? What will you do when faced with groupthink either as an outsider or as part of the group? These are all questions that should guide your reflections.

The three of us firmly believe, based on the contents in this book, you should take action. There are a myriad of things you can get involved with in your organization and social media. Perhaps you could start a blog (or if you already have one, expand) to include reflections on isolation, mindset, mindfulness, and groupthink. This way we can learn from you and your experiences.

Spotlight—*Brad Gustafson*

Brad Gustafson is an elementary principal in Minnesota. He has transformed as a school leader as a result of investing in digital collaboration. He wages a war with isolation every day. Through the use of social media, Brad has built a PLN comprised of friends and colleagues dedicated to student success.

Prior to connecting, he approached his work as an educator similar to many others. He loved his job, was taking graduate classes, enjoyed reading articles and attending conferences, and occasionally telephoned colleagues to seek their input. Although he had established a level of professional trust with educators in his district and state, there remained a lingering sense that education as a profession was inherently isolating.

Fast forward to today, and you'll find that Brad routinely collaborates with educators across the country. The level of connectivity he's achieved disproves the notion that education is an isolating profession. He is utilizing Web 2.0 tools to enhance his leadership capacity, while connecting students to opportunities that were previously unfathomable.

Brad exudes an unparalleled passion for transforming the student learning paradigm. The connections he has made via Voxer, Twitter, blogging, podcasting, and through Google Hangouts have empowered him to more effectively serve students and staff in this digital age.

Twitter-based educational chats are used to continue Brad's professional learning. He has even comoderated a statewide chat for school leaders and aspiring principals with Minnesota's Commissioner of Education. Brad believes that Twitter's power to connect educators to innovative ideas and rock solid resources makes it the single most underutilized tool in all of education. Twitter can also be used to shine the light on the wonderful work students and staff are doing.

Brad never misses an opportunity to share the important work being done by the amazing teachers he serves alongside. Together, they have implemented Mobile Maker Space carts equipped with cutting-edge technology and construction supplies for kids. The 3D printer that is on one of the Mobile Maker Space carts was made possible by donations from DonorsChoose.org. The generous donations that flowed in to fund the 3D printer originated from parents, staff, and even members of Brad's PLN! Furthermore, information about the project was shared with potential donors via social media channels. In the end, it was the students that won as a result of the connectivity of the Greenwood Elementary team.

Their work has been enhanced by virtue of the connections they invest in as a school. Brad estimates that 30 staff members are using Twitter to connect. Greenwood Elementary teachers post tweets to a shared school hashtag called #GWgreats. Their tweets are streamed to two large flat-screen television monitors in the school. This has resulted in greater transparency and an enhanced sense of community. Parents that visit the office often notice the work being done in their children's classrooms. When Brad attends district or state meetings, he's able to stay connected to the important learning because of staff sharing on Twitter. Brad maintains that a school's culture benefits when community, connectivity, and collaboration are valued.

Brad connects with principals across the country to create collaborative student podcasts as well. In the past couple of years, he's collaborated with school leaders Tony Sinanis and John Fritzky to amplify student voice in a global manner. Students from Minnesota, New York, and New Jersey utilized the TouchCast app and produced inspiring videos. They used the hashtag #StuConnect on Twitter to further connect and also encouraged other schools to join a global conversation about education. Last year, a school in Italy participated in one of the cross-state collaborative conversations. A newspaper in Europe wrote about students' global connections and creativity. This year students from 10 states and two countries came together to create a New Year's podcast titled "Big Dreams." These examples of student podcasts would have been inconceivable prior to his becoming a connected educator.

Brad embraces the role of learner with fervor. He continues to leverage digital connections to support the innovative work being done in his school. Brad will be the first to tell you that connecting and collaborating with other schools can be inspiring. However, when it comes to the business of student success and increasing opportunities for kids, he is all business. That's one thing that has not changed about Brad Gustafson since he became connected—Brad is all about "kid wins."

Used with permission of Brad Gustafson.

CONCLUSION

While confidentiality in a school leadership role is a part of the job description, it doesn't have to lead to isolation. You do not have to be plagued by the Gilligan Syndrome. There is a way out, but it will take a little bit of work and open-mindedness from you. We have provided you with a blueprint for building your PLN and your life raft for getting off the Island. Building your PLN allows for new ideas for yourself and your teachers, as well as feedback and even encouragement when you need it most. The amount of time you spend creating initial connections for your PLN will pay back exponentially. We promise.

Jump on Twitter, follow us, and follow the people we have recommended in the appendix. Take one of the hashtags we suggested and just read the tweets. Start interacting when you feel comfortable and all will begin to fall into place. Share with your PLN, share with your staff, and share with your community. Twitter is the 24-hour staff lounge that has exactly what you need, exactly when you need it. Imagine that kind of support the next time you're feeling lonely in your position, and then send us a tweet. We'll gladly help you get going, and we know a lot of other great connected educators who will, too.

As you reflect on the isolation that plagues leaders, it is important to note that it will never go away. Once connected to your PLN, it may become difficult to celebrate others' successes. This is a trap. Everything happens in its own time. In addition, you cannot let yourself become isolated from your day-to-day colleagues since you are connected. We know that sometimes it is easier to send out a tweet, or a Voxer message to your PLN, but you cannot forget about your colleagues. This is the paradox of the modern day school leader.

Reflection and Action

Reflection

Now what? So what? What's next? These three short questions make a quick exit prompt for any staff meeting or PD session, but they also seem fitting for the end of our book.

- Now that you know what you know, so what?
- How can your new learning about being connected help you grow as an educator and a leader?
- What's next for you?

Action

Is connecting each day already a part of your daily habit or do you need to schedule time to check Twitter or blogs so it becomes a habit for you? Did you read straight through the book without stopping to act? Then you'll need to schedule time for yourself to take our suggested action steps to get connected on Twitter, start a Feedly account, or find blogs to learn from. Feel free to tweet out reflections, thoughts, or questions in response to the book using the hashtag #principalpln.

Please do not ever hesitate to connect with one of us with questions or just reach out to connect. We are just a click away:

- @DrSpikeCook, drspikecook@gmail.com
- @PrincipalJ, principaljohnsonj@gmail.com
- @PrincipalStager, principalstager@gmail.com

Resource

PEOPLE WE FOLLOW AND WHY

@CurtRees (Curt): We follow Curt for Response to Intervention (RtI) questions, because his school is a model school for RtI and has presented at a couple of conferences. He is also a tech guru, currently getting his doctorate with an emphasis in technology leadership and was one of the Techlandia Podcast crew. As a principal, he also does a great job of keeping his parents/community well informed through his school Facebook and YouTube channel.

@PosickJ (Jay): His school was one of few that went one-to-one with chromebooks for their fourth to eighth graders, and there are some great tech gurus in his district. He recently ran for the 10,000th day in a row, so he is an inspiration for administrators who claim they don't have time for exercise.

@ReadbyExample (Matt) is an awesome elementary principal focused on literacy and is a grant-writing guru. His blog is filled with incredible information, and he often writes posts for the Stenhouse blog.

@Joesanfelippofc (Joe) is a superintendent doing some incredible work in his district and leading his staff to be connected learners. He cowrote the book *The Power of Branding* and uses the hashtag #gocrickets to share the great things happening in his district.

@twhitford (Tom) is a fellow elementary principal with great ideas, and he is constantly learning with others on twitter.

@Leah_Whit (Leah): Another fellow elementary principal who also happens to be Tom's wife. She is constantly reading, learning, and sharing on Twitter.

@ChadHarnisch (Chad) is a connected high school principal with a great deal of experience and lot of wisdom to share. He recently presented at a conference about how all of his teachers were teaching literacy in the high school—not just the English teachers.

@chadkafka (Chad) is a go-to guy for anything Google, because he is the Google guru! He is also an Apple Distinguished Educator. He used to lead the MobileReach podcast to share all kinds of great apps and advice for integrating mobile devices in education but now has the Teacher Tech Talk Podcast.

@Taml17 (Tammy) joins Chad on the Teacher Tech Talk podcast and shares awesome tech tools/tips. I love following her website to see what she's presenting on.

@pernilleripp (Pernille) started the Global Read Aloud project and is so reflective on teaching in her blog. She is sincerely honest about her practice and gives the classroom back to the students.

@mmiller7571 (Melinda) is a principal from Missouri who used to cohost the Practical Principals podcast that was the inspiration for our PrincipalPLN podcast.

@shiraleibowitz (Shira) and @KathyPerret (Kathy) both comoderate the #Educoach chat with Jessica every Wednesday night. Shira is a rabbi/head of school in New York with a wealth of knowledge on coaching teachers versus just evaluating them. Kathy is a very well-trained instructional coach in Iowa, also with a wealth of knowledge.

@E_Sheninger (Eric) is very well known across the country for having his New Jersey high school utilize social media. He was recognized by the National Association of Secondary School Principals (NASSP) as a Digital Principal Award Winner. You may have seen video clips, news articles, and blog posts about him and his awesome school. He is the author of the book *Digital Leadership*.

@patrickmlarkin (Patrick) was the principal of a Massachusetts high school that has been in national headlines for going one-to-one with huge success (now he's an assistant superintendent). He's also known for being the 2012 NASSP Digital Principal Award Winner.

@8Amber8 (Amber) is an elementary assistant principal in Texas who is constantly sharing great ideas for integrating technology.

@L_Hilt (Lyn) was an elementary school principal in Pennsylvania and is now an Instructional Tech Coach. She is an incredible leader on integrating technology.

@Eduleadership (Justin): A former principal, now director of the Principal Center. He has taught me so many organizational/time management tips to keep up with the crazy amount of workload a principal has.

@Cantiague_Lead (Tony): Principal of an elementary school that has been awarded the National Blue Ribbon Award, was New York State Elementary Principal of the year He cowrote *Power of Branding* with Joe.

@LeaderandReader (Mindy) is an elementary school principal, a true lead learner, constantly sharing her ideas on leadership, leading a literacy school, and Daily 5.

@casas_jimmy (Jimmy): A high school principal full of energy, great ideas and known for being a high school Principal of the Year in Iowa. He started the #IAEdchat to connect the Iowa educators on Sunday nights at 8. pm.

@plugusin (Bill): Bill is a middle school teacher who has written several books and is a phenomenal speaker on PLCs for Solution Tree.

@benjamingilpin (Ben) is an elementary principal who is extremely helpful, motivational, and inspiring. He is an advocate of #michED and creating learning spaces and environments that help students want to learn.

@Joe_Mazza (Joe) is Leadership Innovation Manager at University of Pennsylvania's Graduate School of Education. He has served as an elementary principal, and district EdTech supervisor, and also currently serves as a national family-community engagement advisor to the Institute for Educational Leadership in Washington, DC. He is also the host of #ptchat, a weekly parent-teacher chat on Twitter.

@ideaguy42 (Bob) is Director of Technology and Innovation at a school district in St. Louis, MO, and has also been a middle school principal. He truly is the "IdeaGuy": He shares a ton of wonderful material, is very interactive on Twitter, and is a really fun guy to know and communicate with. His blog is consistently an Edublogs Finalist for "Best Administrator Blog."

References

Beaudoin, M., & Taylor, M. E. (2004). *Creating positive school culture: How principals and teachers can solve problems together.* Thousand Oaks, CA: Corwin.

Boyatzis, R. E., & McKee, A. (2005). *Resonant leadership: Renewing yourself and connecting with others through mindfulness, hope, and compassion.* Boston, MA: Harvard Business School Press.

Brown, B. (2012). *Daring greatly: How the courage to be vulnerable transforms the way we live, love, parent, and lead.* New York, NY: Gotham Books.

Brown, V., & Olson, K. (2015). *The mindful school leader: Practices to transform your leadership and school.* Thousand Oaks, CA: Corwin.

Cookson, P. W. (2005). The challenge of isolation: Professional development— your first year. *Teaching Pre K–8, 36,* 14.

Dussault, M., & Thibodeau, S. (1997). Professional isolation and performance at work of school principals. *Journal of School Leadership, 7*(5), 521–536.

Fullan, M., & Hargreaves, A. (1996). *What's worth fighting for in your schools?* New York, NY: Teachers College Press.

Garmston, R. (2007). Collaborative culture. *Journal of Staff Development, 28*(2), 55–57.

Goleman, D., Boyatzis, R. E., & McKee, A. (2002). *Primal leadership: Realizing the power of emotional intelligence.* Boston, MA: Harvard Business School Press.

Sheninger, E. (2014). *Digital leadership: Changing paradigms for changing times.* Thousand Oaks, CA: Corwin.

Stephenson, L. & Bauer, S. (2010, November 8). The role of isolation in predicting new principal burnout. *International Journal of Education Policy and Leadership, 5*(9).

Whyte, W. H., Jr. (1952, March). Groupthink. *Fortune,* pp. 114–117, 142, 146.

Solutions you want. Experts you trust. Results you need.

AUTHOR CONSULTING

Author Consulting

On-site professional learning with sustainable results! Let us help you design a professional learning plan to meet the unique needs of your school or district. www.corwin.com/pd

INSTITUTES

Institutes

Corwin Institutes provide collaborative learning experiences that equip your team with tools and action plans ready for immediate implementation. www.corwin.com/institutes

ECOURSES

eCourses

Practical, flexible online professional learning designed to let you go at your own pace. www.corwin.com/ecourses

ELIBRARIES

eLibraries

Your online professional resources library. Create a custom collection with more than 1200 eBooks and videos to choose from. www.corwin.com/elibraries

READ2EARN

Read2Earn

Did you know you can earn graduate credit for reading this book? Find out how: www.corwin.com/read2earn

Contact an account manager at (800) 831-6640 or visit **www.corwin.com** for more information